THE PHARAOHS'
CURSE

~~~~~~~~~~~~~~~~~~~~~~~~~~

BY
Susan Dudley Gold

~~~~~~~~~~~~~~~~~~~~~~~~~~

Illustrated
by
Sandy Rabinowitz

CRESTWOOD HOUSE
New York

Library of Congress Cataloging-in-Publication Data

Gold, Susan Dudley.
 The Pharaohs' curse / by Susan Dudley Gold.
    p.   cm. — (Incredible histories)
 Includes bibliographical references.
 Summary: Discusses the sometimes mysterious deaths of well-known archaeologists who have discovered the tombs of
Egyptian pharaohs.
    ISBN 0-89686-511-8
  1. Egyptologists — Death — Juvenile literature. 2. Tombs — Egypt — Juvenile literature. 3. Blessing and cursing —
Juvenile literature. [1. Egyptologists — Death. 2. Curiosities and wonders.] I. Title. II. Series.
 PJ1063.M67   1990
 932'.007202'2—dc20   89-25424
                                                                                                                    CIP
                                                                                                                    AC

Illustration Credits
Cover: Kristi Schaeppi
Interior: Sandy Rabinowitz

Macmillan Publishing Company
866 Third Avenue
New York, NY 10022
Collier Macmillan Canada, Inc.

CRESTWOOD HOUSE

Printed in the United States of America

First Edition

10 9 8 7 6 5 4 3 2 1

Contents

A Treasure and a Curse

In 1922, two Englishmen peered through a hole in a wall of a cave. What they saw would thrill the world. In the room beyond lay piles of gold. Stacked high were golden statues, furniture, chariots, tools, and shrines. They belonged to a young king of Egypt who lived 3,300 years ago. His body, wrapped in linen, lay in the next room, where it had been for many years.

Howard Carter and George Herbert, earl of Carnarvon, had discovered King Tutankhamen's tomb, but only Carter would live to see the king's body. Five months after the find, Lord Carnarvon was dead from a fever caused by an insect bite. He was 57 years old.

Newspaper headlines told the story around the world. People said Carnarvon had been cursed for disturbing the king's tomb. When other deaths were reported, everyone began talking about the curse of the pharaohs.

The Pharaohs of Ancient Egypt

~~~~~~

The pharaohs were powerful Egyptian kings who ruled Egypt from about 3100 to 341 B.C. The kings were thought to be gods. The pharaoh was the supreme ruler, and what he said was law.

The vizier, or high priest, ran the government for the king. Other important people included priests, army officers, and scribes. The scribes kept the records for the other groups. At the lower end of the scale were the peasants, poor farmers who worked the fields for the king. Slaves were at the bottom. They were forced to work in the palace, in the mines, and at other jobs.

Rich Egyptians lived lives of ease. Their houses were built of mud brick with bright paintings decorating the walls. The poorer people did the chores. They washed clothes in the river and planted and harvested grains. They also baked and cooked for the rich.

Since there was no money as we know it, people paid workers with food. The Egyptians had many different foods to choose from. They ate duck, beef, mutton, and

fish, all of which they roasted. To drink, they had wine, beer, and milk. Also on the table were vegetables — lettuce, cucumbers, celery, and beans. For dessert they ate cakes, grapes, dates, and figs. As a special treat, they collected honey from bees.

The Egyptians worshiped many gods. Each town had its own god, but only the pharaohs and priests could go to the gods' temples. After visiting the temples, they told the people what the gods wanted.

Pharaohs in Death

Osiris: Guide to Eternal Life

The ancient Egyptians believed that life did not end with death. They thought that when they died, they would go to the Land of the Dead. There they would join Osiris, god of the dead. If they passed all his tests, they would live forever.

According to myth, Osiris had once been king of Egypt. Osiris's brother, Set, was jealous of the king and wanted to be the pharaoh. He trapped Osiris in a chest, put weights on it, and sank it in the Nile River.

When she found out what Set had done, Osiris's wife, Isis, brought Osiris back to life with her magic. But he decided to stay in the Land of the Dead. He waits there for others who die and guides them to eternal life.

Preparing for the Land of the Dead

The Egyptians took great pains to get ready for life after death. They believed a person could not live after death if the body was not preserved. It took 70 days to prepare the body for its tomb. First it was washed in the Nile River. Then the body was cut open on the left side. The stomach, lungs, liver, and intestines were removed and stored in special jars called canopic jars. The brain was removed by pulling it out through the person's nostrils. It was thought to be worthless and was thrown away.

Wads of linen or spices and gums filled the spaces where the organs once had been. The spices used were ones thought to have been watered by the tears of the gods, crying for the dead Osiris.

The Egyptians left the heart in the body. They believed the heart did the thinking for the body. Later, in

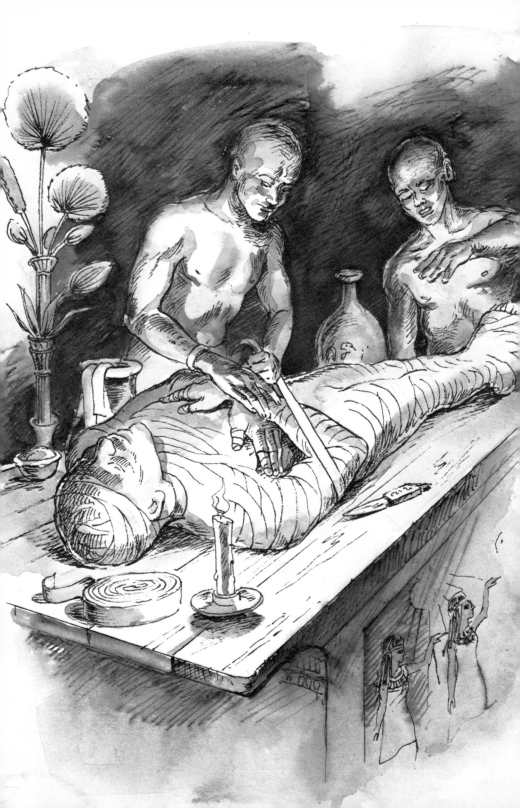

the Land of the Dead, Osiris would look at the dead person's heart to judge whether the person had earned eternal life.

Once the organs were removed, the body was soaked in oil. After two weeks, a special kind of salt (natron) was added to preserve the body.

After 40 days, the body was dried out. Then it was ready for a "beauty" treatment. The skin was rubbed with oils to keep it smooth, and the nostrils were filled so they would keep their shape. One king's body had peppercorns in its nostrils, which experts think were added to renew his sense of smell. The Egyptians also dyed the king's hair red.

Strips of linen were then wrapped around the body. The wrapped and preserved bodies are called mummies. Those putting on the strips wrapped each finger and toe separately. Then they wrapped the arms and legs and the rest of the body. They covered each layer of linen with gum, which hardened the body. While the mummy was being prepared, priests said prayers.

Ramses II was a mighty king who ruled Egypt for 66 years from 1304 to 1237 B.C. When he died, he was covered with cloth that was painted to look like Osiris. The god of the dead had a long, thin beard and eyes lined with black, and he held a snake in his arms for protection.

Jewels and gems were tucked into the mummies of kings and rich Egyptians. Over Ramses' head was placed a golden mask. The Egyptians believed evil spirits tried to stop the dead from reaching the Land of the Dead. To ward off the evil spirits, they buried charms with the body. One special charm — a scarab — was shaped like a beetle and was supposed to bring eternal life. The Egyptians also carved or painted the words of spells on a wooden coffin, or sarcophagus.

Once everything was done, the mummy was put into the coffin. Two women guarded the body until it was buried. Usually, one of the women was the widow of the dead person. The relatives had strong reasons for making sure everything was done right. If something was wrong, the dead person would not be accepted by Osiris. The Egyptians believed the dead person would then come back as a demon and harm them.

The sarcophagus was loaded into a boat built for that purpose. The boat with Ramses' body aboard was pulled by oxen to the Nile. It took two to three weeks to reach the king's burial ground.

Famous Tombs

Ordinary Egyptians buried their dead in vaults or caves in the rock. Kings, thought to be gods, built great monuments for their burial sites. Since death played a major role in the Egyptians' religion, kings spent years getting ready for their burial. During the Old Kingdom, some of the pharaohs built the Great Pyramids for their final resting spots. The pyramids at Giza are probably the world's most famous tombs.

Made of stone, the pyramids soar high above the desert. The Great Pyramid of Giza, built for King Khufu, is more than 400 feet high, taller than a 40-story building.

Inside the pyramids, the Egyptians built rooms for the dead king or queen. Their mummies were placed in one of the rooms deep inside the pyramid.

Other kings hollowed out a series of rooms in the rocks. Some of the tombs at the burial site near Thebes, known as the Valley of the Kings, lay hundreds of feet inside a mountain. Thebes was once the capital city of Egypt. It was at the Valley of the Kings that Ramses II was buried.

Once Ramses' boat landed, the mourners put the coffin on a sled, which oxen pulled to the tomb in the mountains. A second sled carried the jars with the king's organs. Behind the sleds walked the men in the family, joined by officials and friends. Following them were women who wept for the dead king.

Along the path, priests sprinkled milk to please the gods and sprayed incense to make the air smell sweet.

The king's servants walked at the end of the parade, carrying food, clothes, and furniture for his tomb. They also had small statues of servants. These would do the work for the king in the Land of the Dead. At one time, slaves were buried along with their dead king, but later, statues took the place of living servants.

When the group came near the tomb, dancers whirled around the coffin, while musicians sang special songs. Wearing a dog mask, a priest greeted the mummy. He was disguised as Anubis, the dog-headed god, who would guide the king to the Land of the Dead.

Next it was time for the "Opening of the Mouth" ceremony. The priest touched the mummy's nose, eyes, mouth, and ears with an adze, a tool like an ax used to smooth wood. This allowed the dead person to see, smell, taste, and hear in the Land of the Dead. It also let his or her soul be reborn.

Before Ramses was buried, the mourners held a huge feast. The priests said prayers while everyone ate meat, cakes, breads, and fruits. The people hoped the king would have similar meals in the Land of the Dead.

After the feast, the mummy in its coffin was taken to the burial site. Each king had an entire suite of rooms, connected by long passageways, deep in the cliff.

In the outer room of the tomb, statues of the king and the gods stood guard. A passage led into a great hall, where the mummy was laid. Stored in the rooms nearby were all the things the king would need in the Land of the Dead. One room was filled with furniture, another had a table covered with food and drink, and another contained games, weapons, and clothing.

In the Hall of Judgment

The Egyptians believed the dead entered the Land of the Dead through the Hall of Judgment. There, Osiris sat on a throne. The god of the dead himself was a mummy, wearing the mask of a man.

The dead person was put on trial. Forty-two judges, each wrapped as a mummy, listened to the dead person's story. The judges wore feathers (the symbols of truth) on their heads and held knives in their hands.

At the end of the trial, the dead person's heart was put on one side of a scale. On the other side of the scale, Anubis put an ostrich feather. This was a test to see if the dead person had been evil or good during his or her life. If the scales balanced, the person was given a home in the Land of the Dead. If the scales did not balance, a monster stood by, waiting to eat the guilty one.

Digging for Treasure

Hiding from Robbers

The kings went to great lengths to protect their tombs against robbers seeking gold and jewels. They arranged for priests and others to guard their tombs after their deaths.

Built in massive rock, the tombs were hidden in the side of a mountain or within a pyramid. The outer coffins were of heavy stone. When a king died, the priests sealed the lid of the coffin. In the Great Pyramid, they knocked three giant boulders into the passages so no one could enter.

Entrances to the tombs at the Valley of the Kings were hidden, and the tombs could only be reached through deep shafts. The builders made false walls to

fool robbers. In Seti's tomb, the paintings in the outer room weren't finished. This was done to make robbers think the tomb wasn't being used. Mazes in the tombs led to dead ends.

Priests warned people they would be cursed if they bothered the dead. On a priest's grave in Giza is written a warning that anyone who disturbs the grave will have "final judgment before god."

Even so, the lure of gold was too strong to resist. Robbers entered every tomb they could. They bribed guards and tunneled into the tombs at night. They broke through the false walls.

Searching the tombs, they took all the gold and even unwrapped the mummies to find hidden jewels. Sometimes, the robbers died in the tombs, and their dried bodies were found thousands of years later. Some think they were victims of the curse of the pharaohs.

The loyal priests were very upset. They wrapped up the kings' bodies again and put new seals on the tombs, but robbers returned. At last, the priests decided they had to do something to save the mummies. In the middle of the night, they secretly took the mummies of 40 kings and princes and carried them to the cliffs near Thebes. There they lowered the mummies into a deep tomb. Centuries later, a farm boy found the mummies. Among them were King Seti and King Ramses II.

Robbers weren't the only ones to damage the tombs. The ancient Egyptian King Akhenaton removed all signs of the god Amon and replaced them with those of the sun god. Later kings destroyed King Akhenaton's temples and signs.

By 341 B.C., the pharaohs had lost power. The new rulers, who didn't believe in their gods, destroyed the kings' temples and tombs and built their own.

Modern–Day Explorers

In the 1700s, Napoleon Bonaparte became head of the French Empire. Looking for other nations to conquer, he came to Egypt in 1798. He brought a group of scientists along with him.

On a march through Egypt, a French soldier found a strange stone with writing on it. The tablet was found near the town of Rosetta, so it became known as the Rosetta stone.

One section of the stone was inscribed in Egyptian, and another section was written in Greek. The third was a series of pictures and symbols. The "picture writing," the writing of the ancient Egyptians, is called hieroglyphics. Many people had seen the strange writing on tombs and temples, but no one had ever been able to figure out what it meant. The French hoped that the other writings on the stone would help solve the puzzle.

A young Frenchman, Jean François Champollion, looked at the three languages on the stone and soon figured out what the Greek words said. The priests had written a note to the king thanking him for giving money to the temples. Champollion thought the other two parts of the tablet said the same thing, but it took him years to figure out the second part, written in an early Egyptian language. That led him closer to figuring out the key to hieroglyphics.

On September 1822, Champollion ran to his brother in great excitement. "I've got it," he said, and fainted. When he recovered, he wrote a report on how to read hieroglyphics, which he published two years later.

Napoleon's army soon suffered from hunger and disease. In 1799, the French leader fled Egypt, but the scientists stayed. Egypt filled Napoleon's scientists with wonder. Amazed at the giant pyramids, they spent much of their time studying the ancient tombs.

The French scientists worked in Egypt for three years. When they left, they took many old treasures from the tombs to show people in their home countries. Later, an artist who had been with the scientists wrote a book about Egypt, which many people read.

Suddenly, people who had never heard of Egypt before were talking about its tombs and treasures. Many went to Egypt to see the sights for themselves. Rich people in other lands longed to collect Egyptian treasures. Museums wanted treasures for their collections. All were willing to pay money for statues, jewels, and other items.

The demand compelled local people to search tombs for treasures. They sold all they found. They even sold mummies to collectors who wanted to display them. Carrying tools to dig up the ancient tombs, adventurers from other countries came to make their own fortunes. No one thought about the ancient king's wishes not to be disturbed or about the curse on those who disturbed them.

Archaeologists in Egypt

Archaeologists are scientists who study the remains of ancient cultures. When they heard of the ancient treasures found by Napoleon's scientists, the archaeologists came to Egypt. To them, the search for tombs was more than a treasure hunt; it was a search for knowledge. Their finds told them about the people of long

ago. They learned what the ancient Egyptians ate, how they dressed, and what they believed.

The early archaeologists used shovels and picks to dig up their finds. Sometimes they dug at a site just because it looked right. More often, they studied where other treasures had been found and dug near those sites.

Digging was not easy work in the hot desert sun. Local workers often were not skilled and damaged finds. It wasn't easy to find people willing to do the hard work.

Finding and identifying an old tomb was like solving a mystery. Howard Carter, who found King Tut's tomb, followed clues for six years. He knew other kings had been buried near the spot where he was digging. A cup with King Tut's name on it had been found in the area. So had burial pots for King Tut's funeral and pieces of gold leaf with King Tut's name on them.

Carter had to sift through piles of rubble to find King Tut's tomb, but he didn't give up. His patience was well rewarded.

Wanting only big treasure, many of the people digging in Egypt paid no attention to the smaller items. Mummies, small statues, and many other treasures were destroyed.

The best archaeologists studied everything. They took pictures of their finds before they were moved and kept records of where they were found. Carter took ten years to clear out King Tut's tomb. He drew pictures of the treasures as they lay in the tomb. He cleaned and restored them. Everything was labeled and carefully packed.

Not everyone was as careful as Carter. The early explorer Giovanni Battista Belzoni described sitting on mummy bones in a tomb and crushing them. Even when archaeologists were careful, though, some treasures were lost. Sealed in airtight tombs, mummies lasted for 3,000 years. Taken out into fresh air, they turned to dust.

Today, archaeologists have modern tools. They don't have to unwrap mummies to see what they look like. Instead, they use X rays to take pictures of the insides of the mummies. Special X-ray cameras can even take pictures inside the tombs. They can record an artist's sketch underneath a painted picture.

Scientists no longer have to rely on luck to find ancient tombs. Modern machines can detect where large objects are buried. Machines record exactly where the objects are and tell the scientists where to dig.

People now know the importance of ancient treasures. At first, people took all the treasures they could find. Now Egypt has a law that protects the treasures. They cannot be taken from the country. Egypt puts many of its ancient treasures in its own museums.

An Explorer Meets His Death

The Head in the Desert

Life for the early explorers of the tombs was hard indeed. The desert was hot, and medical care was poor. Disease and sickness brought death to many. Greed created many enemies. And there was the curse. Many believed the curse meant death to those who dared disturb the pharaohs' tombs.

Giovanni Battista Belzoni was one of the strongest — and luckiest — of the explorers. In three years, he made astounding finds. He dug up an ancient temple buried in 40 feet of sand. He found the secret entry to a pyramid, and he uncovered royal tombs and mummies.

But his luck ran out too soon. At age 44, he was dead. Fever struck him as he set out to explore Africa, but many think it was the pharoahs' curse that killed him.

Born in Italy in 1778, Belzoni worked as a strong

man in a theater. His act took him all over Europe and beyond. While in Malta, he met a man who talked him into going to Egypt. Once there, he went to see the pyramids and temples of the ancient Egyptians.

He had heard of statues buried in the sand. What he saw was a giant head resting on the desert. Its body and seven other statues lay under 40 feet of sand. He vowed one day to return and dig up the statues.

In 1817, he went back to the statues in the sand, at a place called Abu Simbel. People said he could never do what he hoped to do, but Belzoni proved them wrong.

He dug with his crew in the hot desert sun. For weeks the digging went on. Because of the heat, they could work only until 9 A.M. and after 3 P.M. Food began to run out. The crew fought among themselves and often refused to work.

At last, eight statues rose like ghosts out of the sand. The statues, all of Ramses II, faced each other in a huge hall. They were part of a giant temple built by Ramses. Inside the temple, other statues of the gods and Ramses were seated on giant thrones. All along the walls, ancient artists had drawn figures and battle scenes.

The find thrilled Belzoni. He knew it was very important and hoped it would bring him fame. But others weren't as pleased. As Belzoni left Abu Simbel, one of the members of the boat crew tried to stab him. When he joined his wife, who was staying at another temple, he got a shock. Someone had smashed the stone sculptures he had set aside from another dig. Scrawled on the broken pieces were the words OPERATION CANCELED. Was the curse at work?

Everyone wanted to hear about Belzoni's finds. He and his wife, Sarah, went on a tour of London, where Belzoni spoke about the treasures of Egypt. He became popular, but he soon grew tired of the city. He wanted to travel again.

Belzoni Meets His Fate

In late 1822, Belzoni set off for West Africa. He wanted to find the beginning of the River Niger, but he never got that far. On the boat, he came down with a fever. A week later, Belzoni was dead.

He was buried under a tree near the river. There is no trace today of his grave.

Henry Salt, who had paid for some of Belzoni's trips to the tombs, died of a stomach infection five years later. Salt's young wife had died earlier of fever. Another explorer of the time, Bernardino Drovetti, lived on until 1852. But he was in poor health and died at 76 in a home for the insane.

Were these deaths the work of the pharaohs' curse? It is a question that will probably never be answered.

Amon's Curse

A King's Punishment

A mighty Egyptian king himself fell victim to a curse, according to an ancient legend. Akhenaton, who ruled from 1379 to 1362 B.C., was cursed by the powerful god Amon. Now he is doomed to wander forever. He cannot join the other kings in the Land of the Dead.

The Egyptians believed Amon was the king of the gods. During the reign of Amenhotep III, 1417–1379 B.C., a great temple was built at Luxor to honor Amon. Amenhotep's name, which means "Amon is content," itself honored the god.

When he became pharaoh, Amenhotep's son, Amenhotep IV, turned away from Amon and worshiped a different god called Aten, the sun god.

So strongly did the king believe in Aten that he changed his own name. The pharaoh's new name, Akhenaton, means "It pleases Aten."

Akhenaton and his queen, Nerfertiti, moved the capital of Egypt from Thebes to el-Amarna. The king and his followers took gold from Amon's temples and

used it to build their own temples to Aten. They cut out the name of Amon from the old temples, and in its place they drew the sun disk of Aten.

The king sang a hymn to the people, telling them he could talk directly to Aten. He claimed to be like the god himself.

At Akhenaton's death, the followers of Amon took over again. Angry at the dead king and his god, they destroyed el-Amarna. Once again, Thebes became Egypt's capital city. The people restored the temples of Amon and inscribed them with Amon's name to replace the hated sun disks of Aten.

The priests were the angriest of all. They had been abused by the king, and now they wanted revenge. They put a curse on the dead king's soul so he would forever wander and never find peace.

The Curse Continues

Centuries later, Joseph Lindon Smith and his friends tried to end Amon's curse. They failed and almost died trying.

An artist, Joseph Smith was an expert in ancient Egyptian art. For 50 years, he visited the tombs of the pharaohs. There he copied the old drawings on the walls and painted pictures of the ancient statues and temples. Many times he set up his easel right in a tomb. His wife, Corinna, went with him to the tombs.

While he painted, he learned much about ancient Egypt, including the curse of Amon. To amuse his friends one day in 1909, he decided to put on a play about Akhenaton. Smith wanted to end Amon's curse and free the dead king.

In the play Smith wrote, the king's mother, Queen Tiyi, asks the gods to help her son. At the end of the play, Amon-Ra grants the king a pardon so he can be at peace at last.

The Smiths planned to present the play on the day the king had died centuries before. Other people had said they had seen the king's ghost on that day. The play would be performed at night when the moon was full. The Smiths planned to invite about 30 people to see the play.

The Smiths set up camp at the Valley of the Tombs of the Queens, where some of the queens of ancient Egypt were buried. The tombs were carved into a side of a steep cliff.

Nearby, in Luxor, was the great temple honoring the god Amon. Amid the tombs, the Smiths set up their stage.

Three days before the big event, the actors met on the

stage to rehearse the play. Smith put on his mask, jumped up on stage, and danced around.

Then Hortense Weigall came on stage. As she spoke, a loud burst of thunder sounded, so loud no one could hear her words. Lightning struck nearby, and the wind blew wildly.

Suddenly, rain poured down on the actors, and a fierce wind swept dust clouds over all. Something even stranger happened. Hail the size of small stones fell. No one remembered ever having seen hail there before.

The storm didn't stop Queen Tiyi. She shouted her song into the wind. As soon as she was done, the rain and hail stopped. That night, Hortense Weigall and Corinna Smith slept on a mattress on the floor of one of the tombs. In the night, Corinna Smith had sharp pains in her eyes. Hortense Weigall's stomach hurt.

In the morning, they told Joseph Smith of their dreams. Corinna had dreamed she was in Amon-Ra's temple. One of the statues there had begun to move and had struck her across the eyes. Hortense had had the same dream, but in her dream, the statue had hit her in the stomach.

A day later, almost everyone connected with the play was sick. Corinna Smith was in the hospital with an eye disease, which doctors feared might cause her to go blind. She did get better, but it was a painful time for her.

Hortense Weigall almost died during an operation on her stomach. Joseph Smith suffered from jaundice, an illness that caused him much pain. Hortense's husband, Arthur, was so upset he had a breakdown. He died years later from a strange fever.

The man who played the music for the play didn't get sick, but his mother fell and broke her leg. She had come to see him at Luxor. Two other friends at the rehearsal became ill, too. One had an abscessed tooth, and the other was sick with the flu.

The play was never performed. Some think the curse remains, and Akhenaton still wanders.

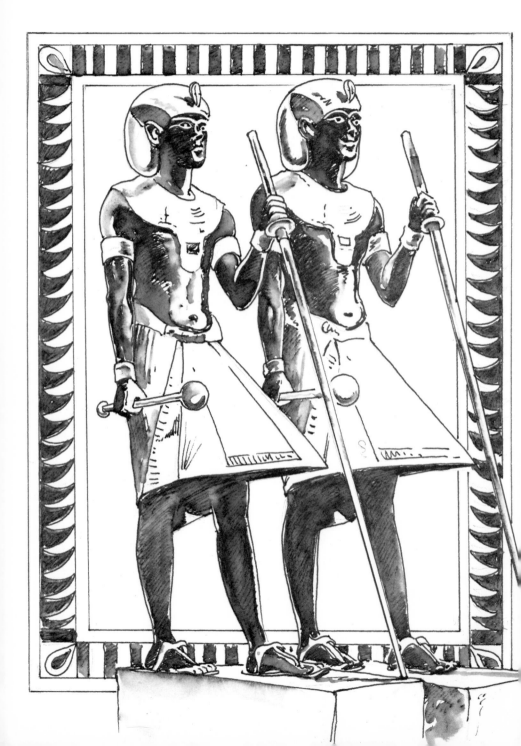

King Tut's Revenge

Wonderful Things

Howard Carter began training as an archaeologist when he was 17. In 1914, Lord Carnarvon, a rich Englishman, hired him. They began digging in the Valley of the Kings two years later.

It wasn't until 1922 that the men found what they were looking for. Below the empty tomb of Ramses II, workers found a step cut into the rock. It was part of a stairway. The steps led to the door, sealed shut centuries before.

Carter knocked a small hole in the door. What he saw took his breath away. The waiting Lord Carnarvon, who could stand the suspense no longer, asked. "Can you see anything?" Carter gasped, "Yes, wonderful things."

The treasures were wonderful indeed. Two life-sized statues of King Tut, made of wood and painted black, guarded the burial room. The eyes and the eyebrows of the statues were of gold.

Chests held the king's clothes — gold sandals worn by the king 3,300 years before, a robe of leopard skin, a gold buckle, and gold rings. Bows and arrows, vases, shirts, and underwear were found in other chests.

A golden throne decorated with gold, glass, and jewels sat waiting for the dead king's return. A scene on the back of the throne showed the young king with his queen.

The rich gold treasures belonged to the young king, Tutankhamen, who ruled Egypt shortly after Akhenaton's reign. Experts think he was only about 18 when he died. At that time, the priests were trying to take control of the country. Some think King Tut may have been killed.

In life, King Tut was a minor figure. His reign was short and his tomb was small compared to others. But in death, King Tut was supreme because of the treasures found in his tomb.

Soon after the king's death, robbers broke into the tomb, but they left in a hurry. Perhaps the priests caught them, or perhaps they were scared off by something. In any case, they dropped the treasures in a pile and ran. They left a jumble of gold piled in the first room of the tomb. That is what Carter saw when he first peeked through the hole in the door.

The priests had resealed the tomb. There is no sign

that anyone else had entered it. Almost all the other tombs had been robbed several times. Ancient Egyptians took the gold, and modern-day looters took whatever else they could find.

They hadn't robbed King Tut's tomb because they couldn't find it, hidden below the tomb of Ramses II.

King Tut's tomb gave experts a close-up look at life in Egypt 3,300 years ago. They learned about King Tut's family life by looking at the paintings in the tomb. They also learned what he wore and the weapons he used. The treasures were a link to life as it was lived centuries before.

A Fearful Curse

People reacted to the discovery of King Tut's tomb with excitement and wonder. But they were also fearful. What powers did a mummy more than 3,000 years old hold?

Lord Carnarvon's death made people even more fearful. Soon after Carnarvon died, Arthur Mace, an American archaeologist, died in the same hotel. George Jay Gould, a friend of Carnarvon, went out to look at the tomb, and the next morning he, too, was dead. Doctors said he died from fever, possibly the plague.

The newspapers reported each death in big headlines. They kept a count of the deaths of all those connected to King Tut's tomb. The death toll: more than 30 people.

Howard Carter didn't believe in the curse. He had spent more time in the tomb than anyone else, and he was alive and well. But other people — even some of the archaeologists — believed a curse existed.

Still a Mystery

If there was no curse, what caused all the deaths? Why did so many of those who visited the tombs become ill? What happened to all the people in Joseph Lindon Smith's play? Some say the strange happenings were just coincidence. People have offered many reasons for the bizarre events:

Fungus — One theory is that fungus in the tombs caused fever. Many of those who died suffered from fever.

Poison — Another idea is that ancient priests used poison to protect the dead. In the airtight tombs, the poison stayed potent. When people opened the tombs and touched the things inside, the poison was released. In some cases, the poison led to death.

Bacteria — Several explorers died of pneumonia, which can be caused by bacteria. According to some people, the mummies bred germs that could cause people in the tombs to become ill.

Mind power — Many people knew of the curse placed on the tombs. When they became sick, they blamed the curse. The thought that the curse would harm them might have made them sicker. In some cases, people even might have been scared to death by the curse.

No doctors — The conditions in the tombs weren't healthy, and many of the tombs were far away from knowledgeable doctors. When people became sick, they might die because of poor medical care.

Coincidence — Many think the deaths had nothing to do with the curse. They say some of the people who died never even saw the tombs. People made up the stories to sell newspapers or because they wanted to tell a good tale.

Scientists offer their own proof that the curse is not to blame. They say many of the tomb explorers lived long lives. Joseph Lindon Smith spent more than 50 years in the tombs, and he lived to be 87. Sir W. M. Flinders Petrie was 89 when he died. That famous archaeologist had spent most of his life in the tombs.

Howard Carter also seemed to have escaped the

curse. He died at age 66, 17 years after finding King Tut's tomb.

Some of those who died had been sick before. Lord Carnarvon had been ill for years before King Tut's tomb was found.

Others died of illnesses common in Egypt, such as eye diseases and fevers.

But many of the happenings remain a mystery. Scientists have been unable to find reasons for them all. And there are those who wonder if the curse remains.

For Further Reading

Aliki. *Mummies Made in Egypt*. New York: Crowell, 1979.

Casson, Lionel. *Ancient Egypt*. New York: Time Life Books, 1965.

Coatsworth, Elizabeth Jane. *Bess and the Sphinx*. New York: Macmillan, 1967.

Cottrell, Leonard. *Land of the Pharaohs*. Cleveland, Ohio: World Publishing Co., 1960.

Honour, Alan. *The Man Who Could Read Stones: Champollion and the Rosetta Stone*. New York: Hawthorn Books, 1966.

Linsner, Kenneth Jay. *Wrapped for Eternity: The Story of the Egyptian Mummy*. New York: McGraw-Hill, 1974.

Macaulay, David. *Pyramid*. Boston: Houghton Mifflin, 1975.

Milton, Joyce. *Secrets of the Mummies*. New York: Random House, 1984.

Mozley, Charles. *The First Book of Tales of Ancient Egypt*. New York: Franklin Watts, 1960.

Pace, Mildred Mastin. *Pyramids: Tombs for Eternity*. New York: McGraw-Hill, 1981.

Payne, Elizabeth. *Pharaohs of Ancient Egypt*. New York: Random House, 1964.

Perl, Lila. *Mummies, Tombs, and Treasure: Secrets of Ancient Egypt*. New York: Clarion Books, 1987.

Swinburne, Irene and Laurence. *Behind the Sealed Door: The Discovery of the Tomb and Treasures of Tutankhamen*. New York: Sniffen Court Books, 1977.

Index